FEELINGS OF THE HEART

FEELINGS OF THE HEART

BY

MARK MAGEE

BOOK MARK PUBLICATIONS
61 Chingford Road Walthamstow London E17 4PW

Date of Publication
August 1997

Published in the UK by
Book Mark Publications
61 Chingford Road
Walthamstow
London E17 4PW

Telephone 0181 923 6183

Printed by:
ProPrint
Riverside Cottage
Great North Road
Stibbington
Peterborough PE8 6LR

ISBN: 0 9528040 77

CONTENTS

'AN ANGEL'

My love! My love! Anne now lies at rest
As loved since time began her life on earth was short,
And her love here, ever blest.

A loving mother ever true children four,
She reared, now in Heaven, eyes still blue,
Her blessing on her children geared.

We that are left are saddened years forty-six - so short,
In our hearts are gladdened by the example her sweet life taught.

And with the Angels, high above Anne's spirit guiding those so loved,
Cancer... she suffered for so long at peace .. with Angels
Who sing her song.

John Ainsley

This poem is dedicated as a tribute
to a loving wife and mother 1980

NATALIE AT SWEET SIXTEEN

Encompass to admire with more than just a glance
An angel's face with deep brown eyes,
Statuesque, and royal deportment,
Lithesome limbs, that beauty beckons to enhance
With graceful steps, in rhythmic dance.
Talent ne'er saw I or any that denies,
Rewarding in all things she tries.
Her heart and soul is mine to dream perchance?
The stars at night may shine as bright
Or, the moon so calm, be splendid!
Quality is more than just a pleasing sight,
As she perfects her ways as young women ever did.
That Natalie, with all her girlish might,
Transcends all before her, as my delightful grandest kid!

Ron Amato

TEENAGER

A child is born
From one's own seed
And through the summer's sun
And winter's bleak
The years pass by
As clouds with no less heed.

From babe to girl
And into teens
I've seen her grow,
And yet to understand
But why! A generation parts.
Who am I to interfere
For she is here now
And pleasure, is to touch her hand.

The future that awaits in time
Will part us as is destiny.
But joy, will stay sincerely.
Am I not a lucky man!
For parent love binds dearly!

Ron Amato

3

LOVE OF A SPECIAL KIND

When you meet your true love, don't you go overboard.
One thing you want to do is spend everything you can afford,
Nothing is too much to make the relationship closer,
For this is for sure, and it will last for ever,
One doubt only in your mind
Will the return of love, be of the same kind.

Time brings reassurance in that delight,
As a deeper love develops, as is only right.
The love gets stronger day by day,
And material things get less in every way,
For a serious commitment is blossoming
Which may be a sharing of a ring.

Sharing experiences in every direction,
Brings joint love nearer, with great affection.
The next big step is to decide on marriage,
Here you need family support and love to encourage,
For when the final day is fixed
It's essential that both families are happy and not mixed.

The following days are like a trial of love,
Testing you out to see if you are a dove.
Needless to say if you trust each other
You will come through this test with flying colour,
Love has no bounds in matters like this,
For you can only end up in marital bliss.

But true love does not end at the alter you know,
For your life we trust, has a long way to go,
To make the world a better place for those who follow,
Your children should share the love you hallow.
So as a final thought before we leave,
Hold on to that love we receive.

Ralph Andrews

4

LOST LOVE

I walked upon the sea shore
Once more again to see
My sweet and lovely darling
As she walked away from me.

I could hear her happy laughter
My waiting was in vain,
The echo coming back to me,
Above the wind and rain.

One day I'll know the reason
Was I most to blame?
I still can hear her laughter
Above the wind and rain.

I will always be there waiting
For ever if need be
With open arms I'll stay
Until she at last returns to me.

Barbara Appèl

I dedicate this poem to
lovers everywhere.
Feelings are a precious thing.

LOVE BUG

You came into my life so unexpectedly,
When you moved into the empty house, across the road to me,
I have seen you watching me from your window, when I go walking
Past.
And I find that I walk slowly now, where as I used to walk quite fast.

And when we met by chance in the car park, and you gave me a kiss
And a hug.
I knew there was no mistaking, I had been bitten by that old love bug.
My legs just turn to jelly, when I hear you speak my name.
And I know that for me at least, life will never be the same,
You have put me in a quandary, and I don't quite know what to do,
You see I am over fifty Jack, and you are just coming up to two.

Maureen Arnold

This poem is dedicated to Kerry and Paul
Who's little boy Jack is my Love Bug.

ORMOND STREET

Walk down Ormond Street feel the pain
Go into the hospital and feel the same
See the children's faces most happy and gay
For only at Ormond Street do these children stay.

Children are playing and living in pain
They're fighting so hard to be well again
The doctors and nurses love them all
Physiotherapist help them walk.

The surgeons repair them with gentle hands,
They use their knowledge and skills, even pray
For the children of Ormond Street who stay each day.
Some children recover, some children remain
These children are special in every way.

This place is special this place is safe
For children with illnesses which others can't save.

Some children remember, some children forget
But most remember the love they met.
In doctors and nurses who work each day
To save these children in every way.

Most children recover, the lucky ones, have been
Touched with caring and loving hearts.

The memories of children who slipped away are never forgotten,
And we pray one day that doctors and surgeons will have the
Skills to heal them all, then all will be well.

For children are special you must agree
They're worth the pleasure they give and we receive
So send a donation for special research
And help these children live as they deserve.

Our son recovered a fight he gave
A year of worry Ormond Street took away
My heart is saddened for children I saw
They fought so hard but were no more.

Their little faces I'll not forget.
For now I only have one regret,
I wish I was God to heal all I have met.

Susan Aspinall

This poem is dedicated to my son Martin Aspinall.
Who had the strength to survive heart surgery (three times)
To the doctors and nurses of Great Ormond Street Children's Hospital
Whom never gave up on Martin during his year long fight.

FAMILY SECRETS

My inner feelings bubbling
I cannot share them round
The joy of my relationship
The love I've finally found
I hold within my feelings
The pride so full within
To try to tell somebody
Oh where would I begin
My husband is my backbone
He's there if I should call
He's there to wipe away my tears
He's seen me through it all
My life has been tormented
A secret that's never told
But now I have my husband
He's there for me to hold
Yet still my inner feelings
Are not completely out
But no longer do they haunt me
I no longer scream and shout
My husband's there to talk to
He's really there for me
But my feelings are still smouldering
Locked up with me as a key.

Dawn Avery

This poem is dedicated with love to
Keith Avery.
Greatest love XX

AUTISTIC CHILD

A distant look held in his face,
Autistic child, he has no place.
Fear of all he looks upon,
Screams, no tears, he knows no wrong.
Fighting life through innocent eyes,
His parents in vain calm the cries.
Disabled in mind, yet cannot be seen,
To fantasise or have no dream.
To give him love, another fight,
To teach him wrong, as well as right.
A beautiful face is all you see,
A mind locked up, you hold no key.
Understand, or at least to try,
The autistic child, an emotionless cry.

Dawn Avery

*This poem is dedicated to
our son Aston Martin Avery.
One day you will understand.*

A CHILD'S OBSESSION

My head is filled with illusions, my sleep is plagued with dreams
My nightmares are more vivid and louder are my screams
My tears fall more often, upon my carpet floor
As I think I hear your footsteps, approach my open door.

I'll never forget that night, when you did disregard my age
And even though I protested, you stamped my empty page.
So I lost my prized possession, because my sanity had flown,
Because of a child's obsession, my virginity now you own.

And now I feel ugly, unloved, unwanted and used
As my manner kind and flirty, you simply just abused
And now you have gone, you left me on my own
Listening for your voice, and waiting by the phone

I know that I love you, I guess I always will
But trying to regain my feelings, is to climb a vertical hill
So I pray that you'll come back, that one day you'll return
But until that sun is risen, my heart is left to burn.

Janine Ayres

OUR DAY

You are my best friend
And our relationship will never end
In one week's time we'll be husband and wife
And we'll be in love for the rest of our life.

Beyond my life, my body and soul
To love you forever is my only goal
For richer and poorer, to honour and obey
The 18th of December will be our special day.

To me there is no other that lives
To me you have everything, and this you give
If you have got it you make sure it's mine
Your love, your happiness and your time.

Tracey Barrett

Dedicated to my husband Paul Barrett
Who has given me lots of inspiration and support.

TREASURE

Darling - let me tell you about treasure
It's not as you'd suppose - Silver and Gold.
Treasure is a love you cannot measure
Treasure is a joy that you can hold -

Safe within your heart - when you are weary
A thought to brighten up your darkest day.
A thing of beauty, you see very clearly
The joy that's in a baby at its play.

Treasure is a thing that men seek after
Seek -but seldom find it - that is true.
Yet it is found within a baby's laughter
And comes in little packages - like you.

Irene Beattie

Dedicated to my Grandsons Stephen and Paul Bryans

THE FIRST TIME I FELL IN LOVE

The first time that I fell in love - is very real to me,
I remember I would run to him, to sit upon his knee.
I'd throw my arms around his neck, my head upon his chest,
And vow that he would always be - The one I'd love the best.

He wasn't always kind to me - sometimes he would tease,
But because I loved him so, I did my best to please.
We had such happy times together - one thing I would like
Was when he gave me rides upon the crossbar of his bike.

He bought me lots of silly things that gave me endless joy,
Like Easter eggs with dolls inside or some ridiculous toy.
And he took time to talk to me - for he was that sort of boy.

He'd meet me from his place of work, and then walk home with me.
And though he looked at other girls - he said he just loved me.
Then I saw him kiss the girl next door - I didn't know what to do,
I thought! He loves her more than me - it broke my heart in two.

Yes! The first time that I fell in love - I vowed I'd have no other.
But I was only eight years old,
And he was my big brother.

Irene Beattie

This poem was written for my brother.
Sadly he was killed in Holland Sept. 17th. 1944

ERNIE MY LAD

What are you doing here - Ernie My Lad
When you were too young to die?
Too young to lay neath cold dark earth
Unable to see the sky -

Unable to feel the gentle breeze
As it softly caressed your brow.
When you laughed and played in childhood days
But what are you doing now?

Are you thinking of man's intolerance
Lack of love for his fellow man.
That cut you off in your prime of life
As it has since time began.

I see the poppies that dance at your feet
I know you were just twenty three.
I think of us - who loved you and lost
And how empty our lives will be.

As we softly touch your photograph
Then sit alone and cry.
Choked that we couldn't kiss your cheek
Or be there to say good bye.

You fought and you fell on this battlefield
Mid the blood - the tears - and the sweat.
While we pray to God who loves us all
For we can never forget.

That you left your home - and died alone
And only God knows why.
Oh what are you doing here Ernie My Lad?
When you were too young to die.

Irene Beattie

Written for my beloved brother Ernie Kelly 2nd Devons
Killed September 17th 1944 (interred in Holland)

MUM

A person who I care for most,
Is always there somehow.
Listening, loving.
Holding me close,
No matter what or how.
She doesn't hate,
She always loves,
So kind and precious too.
I love her dearly
Oh, so much,
I love you Mum,
I do.

Kimberly Berry

MIRACLE

The power of the light, it burned deep in my soul,
The strength that it has given me, has filled the gaping hole.
I feel that I am one again, free from all that binds,
I feel I could do anything - defy all space and time.
Something must have saved me, I thought my time had come,
Looking down from high above everything and everyone.
I saw myself just laying there, people huddled round,
The sirens getting closer as I bled there on the ground.
The further that I rose, the less that I could see,
Surely this was all a dream - it surely was not me.
It was then the miracle happened, everywhere became so bright,
I felt a warmth inside of me, it must be from the light.
Then I woke in hospital, at first it felt quite odd,
Now I describe my experience as the day I was touched by God.

Amanda Brind

TALL, DARK

Tall, dark and handsome, the fairy tale kind,
You know me by heart - read my mind.
You can guess what I'm thinking by a glance at my eyes,
Brush off my sarcasm - but that won't die!

That sharp sense of humour, and cute sideways grin,
Rolled up into one, how lucky I've been.
These feelings I've got - they're strange and so new,

Deep,

Strong,

True,

Perfection...that's you.

Amanda Brind

*This poem is dedicated to
my husband Kevin.
I'll love you always.*

YOUR TRUTH...

Stop...and listen to the steady beat of your heart...
Pause...wait...and feel your pulse in your head...
Slowly...you draw me near, take your hand in mine
I feel my breath quicken as you tell me what you feel
As you hold me,
As you take my heart

Waiting...feeling the warmth of your breath on my lips...
Knowing...for certain the way you feel about me...
Slowly...You put your arms around me
And here I am
Suspended in time.

Carly Brown

This poem is dedicated to Rob

THIS LETTER

This letter's just to say that I don't love you any more.
It's not your fault, it's just I find there's nothing left to say.
I still remember our first date, the movie that we saw
And the time we went to Saundersfoot on holiday.

I'll never be able to forget the first time we kissed,
Or when we won a prize for dancing at our local club.
I know your favourite drink's Martini with a lemon twist.
It took me months to master your trick with the Camel stub.

On the 'phone the other night we talked about all this:
In fact, our past is all we ever talk about these days.
All we have in common are our memories of bliss.
That's not enough, it's time for us to go our separate ways.

Don't be sad - sooner or later, everything must end.
Remember you can always count on me to be a friend.

Christopher Bryant

TO THE ONE I LOVE

I dreamt of you last night as I lay there asleep
We were on a deserted beach
But we could hear our song playing in the distance
The cool summer night was coming to an end.

I knew the night I'd never forget
We walked and talked for hours and hours
The waves were gently lapping in and gently lapping out,
The seagulls were sending mating signals to each other.
The way you looked in the midnight moon
Made me realise how much I loved you.
We looked around as we did our eyes met,
We knew that time was on our side as we kissed.

I woke just before the sun was to rise,
And I remembered the dream I had just had
I felt sad to begin because I wanted the dream
To go on forever.
But as I looked at you laying there
So sweet, so gentle,
I woke you up and we watched the sun rise together.

To the one I love

Sarah Burrows

This poem is dedicated to
John Sharratt I will always love you.

ON BEING IN LOVE

Seeing eyes
Measure carefully
Before softening into
That certain smile
Which will make
Just one minute
Worth a week.

I wonder if my life's better part
Didn't happen during just one romance's
Crazy patchwork quilt of emotion
Completely summarising all I ever was.
If I became too old
To fall in love again
I want to die.

Andrew Challen

WHY

It was never meant to be this way
The emptiness and sadness throughout everyday
I was supposed to be happy and full of joy
But that was before I lost my little boy.

When does the hurting stop and the pain disappear
When again will laughter be here
Day in, day out, it's just the same
Full of bitterness and anger, sorrow and pain.

I want to cry, but the tears don't fall
I am hitting my head against the same brick wall
Why did this happen, was it really meant to be
It just doesn't make any sense to me.

Weeks have passed, but the pain gets stronger
The days seem short, but the nights are longer
I see your face when I close my eyes
I imagine you are here, beside me you lie.

I hear you cry, so I hold you tight
I cradle you in my arms, I'll hold you all night
I open my eyes, but you I cannot see
You are no longer laying here with me.

I look around, but you're not here
I begin to cry, it's just not fair
Could this all be a terrible dream
I pinch myself and then I scream.

Why did this happen? What did I do
I had so much love to give to you
We didn't have much time together
And now it's too late, you are gone forever.

Sarah Chapman

CONNOR

You were with us for such a short while
We never saw your smile
We never heard you laugh or cry
And now it's time to say goodbye.

You were perfect in every way
There was so much we wanted to say
There was so much we wanted to do
We had so many plans for you.

We could only stroke your fingers or tickle your toes
How we wanted to hold you close
You were so tiny, but put up a fight
But all that suffering wasn't right.

Those few days were precious and dear
How we wish that you were still here
You will be in our thoughts daily
And never be forgotten, especially by Hayley.

And so my darling it's time to rest
Goodnight Connor and God bless.

Sarah Chapman

MEMORIES

The dream, that was yours and mine
Way back in another time
Walking hand and hand
Bare foot through the sand
There was only you and me
No one else, could we see
On a cold and frosty night
Forsythia blossoms were in sight
Gazing at the moon, through the trees
Shivering from the cold night breeze
As you held me close, we kissed
You whispered, memories are made of this

But soon came the storm
All our loyalties were torn
For neither of us were free
So our love, just couldn't be
The world, of you and me
And all that we had planned
Fell like grains of sand
The time came for us to part.
You knew, with you went my heart
And as you kissed, me dear
You whispered, I'll always be near
Our love, could never die
You felt, the same as I.

K. Priddes Coggins

25

MY HUSBAND, MY LIFE

I loved my husband Doug
I know my Doug loved me,
He gave me hope
He gave me strength
He gave me joy Heavenly sent,
He gave me yesterday
And the stars above.
He gave me his name
And his love.
The warmth of his smile
The bliss from his kiss
A hug with his arms
He had so much charm.
His loving arms that held me so tight
Made me peaceful and everything right.
I miss my darling Doug who's now in Heaven,
He's so far away, so high above,
He's with the Angels and Jesus' love.
He's again happy, I know this is true
For he's with the animals he once knew,
For nature to him was a beautiful thing
I miss him so much
With his tender touch.
So I now pray every day
For my special day to be with him,
To be in his arms once again
Then I'll no longer need to cry
For I'll be there by his side.

Valerie Colbert

I dedicate this poem to a loving husband, friend and father
Who I love and miss very much.
I now sleep with his memory, while he now sleeps with the Angels.

UNANSWERED QUESTIONS

How can it feel like yesterday
And yet, an eternity?
Since, we two together shared life so
Happily.

How can it be that the sun still shines,
That the flowers bloom that children play?
Life for me, so empty now, I miss
You more every day.

Happy, laughing people everywhere, two by two,
Or so it seems.
While I try to go forward, but never forget
The years which now feel like dreams.

For you will always be a part of me and
I will be a part of you.
I'll honour and cherish the memory
In all I say and do.

I want to cry, to shout, to rave, give
Way to my heart, full of pain.
But my tears won't flow, and I am left
Helpless, alone again.

Jean Collins

*This poem is dedicated to
George in memory of a lifetime of happiness together,
and who I will miss for the rest of my life.*

HOW LOVELY

While we listened to the music
I saw your face shine with brightness
And in return
I listened to the tune -

It opened my heart
And it was filled
With sweet melodies;

They took the form and shape
Of words I would have liked to say
But none came over my lips
Except -

I looked at you and said:
'How lovely!'

Margrit Dahm

This poem is dedicated to Rina

MY ONE MY ONLY LOVE

You light up my life
You bring me joy
You've given me so much
Including our darling boy
You are my sunshine
Shining through the rain
Through all the tough times
You have eased the pain
Even though times are hard
It's on you I depend
You are my lover
As well as my best friend
All you do is struggle
Working hard as can be
So that we are clothed and fed
And there's always food on the table for tea
I just want you to know you're my saviour
My life would be empty without you
You help to ease my worries and fears
You are goodness through and through
At the end of the day when night draws in
And outside it's windy and cold
I know you'll be there by my side
To comfort and to hold.

Paula Daines

This poem is dedicated to
Steve James, the man who gives everything
and expects nothing in return.
'My one my only love'
Forever

LAST FEELINGS

Your touch made me melt
Your lips were so warm
Our bodies embraced
Our love had been born.

My heart beated fast
My head felt light
As you kissed me softly
As day turned to night.

We savoured the passion
We breathed in the air
The night was all ours
The love we could share.

It all went so fast
It was finally over
I had to leave you, but
I will still love you, forever.

Gemma Davis

I NEED YOU

I need you with me
To help me stand tall
To face what's in front of me
To catch me when I fall.

I need you with me
When I want to cry
When life is low
When things around me die.

I need you with me
Just to be sure
Just so I know your there
Just to guard the door.

I need you with me
So I can be strong
So we'll be together
So things won't be wrong.

I need you with me
Because I do
Because your the one for me
Because I love you.

Gemma Davis

1954

Do you remember when we met?
You must know it was spring.
We had a lot of fun that year,
So much I wanted to sing.

About the lovely time we had,
When summer came around,
The sun shone brightly every day,
We enjoyed the love we'd found.

In the autumn, the days were short,
The weeks went by quite fast,
Lots of films and shows to see,
We knew our love would last.

And in the winter Christmas came,
Along with frosty weather,
And by the time new year arrived,
We know we'd stay together.

Marion Denmark

*This poem is dedicated to
my lovely husband Ronald
1922 - 1997*

ANOTHER PLACE, ANOTHER TIME

You're always full of fun,
Telling jokes, teasing everyone,
When you are near I always smile,
I miss you if I don't see you for a while.

I only have to think of you,
To cheer me up when I am blue,
I think of all the stories I have told,
They warm me up when I am cold.

When you're sad, you never show,
To people around you're feeling low,
But, in my heart I feel your pain,
I want to hear you laugh again.

Knowing you has bought me so much pleasure,
Thoughts of you I'll always treasure,
I cherish the moments we spend together,
I know it can't be forever.

There is a special place for you in my heart, you see,
But, it just was not meant to be,
Perhaps in another place, another time,
I would have tried to make you mine.

Claire C. Dobson

WITHOUT YOU!

Away from you I felt so alone,
I keep telling myself if only I'd known,
What life would be like without you by my side,
My feelings for you are so strong, so deep, so why did I lie?

When I'm not with you I feel empty and cold,
No-one near me to reach out and hold,
Inside my heart black clouds roll by and the thunder roars,
The rain keeps coming, it pours and pours.

Thinking of you breaks my heart again,
Eyes full of tears, they show my pain,
I suffer from the hurt that you feel, too,
Please believe me when I say I love you.

I'm scared I may lose you forever,
I want us to be always together,
You turn me on with all your charms,
At last I'm back within your arms.

Without you my life would never be the same,
I promise I'll never hurt you again,
I will always carry you in my heart,
I know, now, we shall never part.

Claire C. Dobson

This poem is dedicated to
my husband Colin.

WE HAVE SOMETHING VERY PRECIOUS...

I am reminded of that
Whenever I am away from you
Busy doing something
And you drift into my mind
Making me smile inside.

I realise it
When we're together with others
And I watch your face
And listen to your voice
And I can hardly wait
Until we're alone together
Because being with you
Is all I really need....

I am sure of it
When I hold you near me
Two people, two hearts
Joined as one
And I feel so complete
And so happy
Aware that with you
Is where I always want to be.

Love you, babe.

Adrian Docherty

SHERYL MY DAUGHTER

S is for sweet child, born on the Sabbath day,
H is for helpfulness, which you openly display,
E is for efficient, a quality of yours clearly seen,
R is for refined, something you have always been,
Y is for youthful in countenance, no matter how old you grow,
L is for lovely - which you are, although you refuse to believe it I
                                                              know.

M is for mine, you're my precious gift from God above,
Y is for yoke, we are joined with a special kind of love.

D is for dear, because that's what you are,
A is for ability, its clearly seen that you're a star,
U is for understanding, you always listen and try to understand,
G is for gem, beautiful and precious gem; giving a guiding hand,
H is for humorist, making people laugh is a road that you have trod,
T is for tenacious, in many things; especially your love for God,
E is for enigma, people can never truly work you out,
R is for resourceful, that's something you are without a doubt.

Doreen

Dedicated to my loving daughter Sheryl

36

LIFE

I've lived my life for thirteen years
And I've had my share of painful tears
Something's go right and something's go wrong
But every time my feelings grow strong.

My friends would be there by my side
And always comfort me once I'd cried
Something's were silly, something's were not
Some I'd remember others forgot.

Some of the years I'd like to relive
Some of the years I'd like to forgive
I love my friends and family and I think they know
Although I've never let my feelings show.

I can be nice I think you'll find
All of my life I've tried to be kind
I want to grow up but not to fast
I want all my memories of childhood to last.

I want to wake up on a bright Christmas morning
With children saying thank you, opening presents and yawning
When I grow old and in elderly years
I'll pray to God to tell Him I have no fears
When I die the sky cloudy and blue
The message in my mind will be I love you.

Kirsty Anne Dunn

This poem is dedicated to
my late Grandad 'Wag'

A MOTHER'S LOVE?

As I look down at you my heart fills with pride,
But all the love I have for you I know I'll have to hide,
For society has made my choice and this I have to do,
So I write this letter to you and hope you'll see through
The hatred you could feel for me and know my words are true.

I didn't know your father for very long you see.
And when I told about you he decided to set me free
A wife and family he already had, he then decided to declare
And to take me on with you he didn't think was fair.

And so you see he let me go, alone again was I
I turned then to my family but to keep them, you I must deny
I knew right then to be on my own and never be a wife
Wasn't the right thing for you, you deserve a better life.

I love you more than life itself but to keep you would be wrong
So as I gave you up to them I had to stay strong
A lovely couple came for you to take you to their home
And once again here I am empty and alone.

I hope you understand me son, when you read this when you're older
I tried to do the best for you my love is growing warmer not colder
Two loving parents you truly deserve and I hope they filled the gap
But remember I'll always love you that's unconditional and on tap.

So this is where I'll end it
But somewhere deep inside
I hope one day we'll meet again
And my love for you I'll no longer need to hide.

Tracy Earey

MY HEART, MY HURT

He was my gentile
He knew a Jew
My dilemma was love
but what did the label say.
I got too drunk on old wine
That spirit took me to a dangerous place,
Where another spirit found me
........and I got drunk on
....LOVE, IS GOD IS....LOVE.

Lisa Ellis

THE SEAGULL

White Flutter
gently as babies eye lids opening
landed by my path as I walked to the front office of the school.

I've brought you your presents
prayers of your mother, written this morning to you.

I smiled within, and let the soaring freedom leave on white sails.
And as I looked at the sky I saw the thoughts of all who love me....
As the Universes' arch

SURROUNDING ME....

Lisa Ellis

This poem is dedicated to
my Mother Ilse Heibel

RELATIONSHIPS

Sixty two and wed for more than half my life,
I've fallen in love again, not with my wife,
Our love is eternal until we both die,
Can a man have two loves? I know I must try.

So natural, so young, like my wife reborn,
I felt terribly guilty between them torn,
It's early days and her feelings I don't know,
But there is something and I'm sure it will grow.

Not very chatty, I make all the running,
Though she does respond, is she being cunning?
Our humours the same it's nice to amuse her,
With a gorgeous smile I could not but choose her.

Hair of bright gold, no particular style,
How I long to enfold her just for a while,
Quite shortish and plump for she does have her faults,
But that smile, and those eyes, my heart somersaults.

The clothes that she wears they don't really flatter,
In places she looks decidedly fatter,
She's rather too young for impeccable taste,
But no matter how pretty, girls still need a waist.

She refuses to walk whether near or far,
That may cause problems for I don't have a car,
But if she feels for me as I do for her,
She will learn to walk and I wouldn't demur.

I'm rambling on so with more bad points than good,
On reading back it doesn't sound as it should,
So in black and white with words that don't falter,
I really do love my darling Grand-daughter.

And I can't wait for the day I'll hear her say,
With that smile on her face, in her own sweet way,
Looking straight in my eyes as young children do,
With a hug and a kiss 'granddad I luv yoo!'

Charles Elsey

This poem is dedicated to Lauren
'Three Times Over The Moon'

IN LOVING MEMORY

I saw you wince today,
But you said not to fret.
The pain wasn't unbearable,
I wanted to believe you and yet.
As I sat there silently watching,
I felt your agony creeping.
Where brave souls keep up the fight,
Love lies gently weeping.

Was it really only yesterday?
Well that is how near it seems.
That I met you in the dance hall,
The answer to all of my dreams.
We've loved and supported each other,
Through fifty years good times and bad.
You've been my friend and my lover,
I give thanks, rejoice and am glad.

I sit by your bedside for hours,
As you sleep I take hold of your hand.
I marvel at how you've kept going,
And wonder how much more you can withstand.
But suddenly I know that it's over,
I feel you slip quickly away.
'I love you my darling'. I whisper,
Knowing we'll be together some day.

Barbara Eyre

PERFECTION

Roaming the winding pathways,
.Together, hand in hand,
Lingering awhile, the land to view,
By the style we stand.

A wondrous sight surrounds us,
No need for any words,
The breeze so gentle on our cheeks,
Plus the song of the birds.

Heaven is all about us,
The silence is sublime,
What a wondrous thing this love be!
This love of yours and mine.

We turn to face each other,
Into your arms I fly,
In your embrace, your need of me,
Murmuring a sigh.

A sigh of sweet contentment,
My searching is all done,
Our lips do meet in kisses sweet,
And we two are one.

To roam the fields and byways,
Together hand in hand,
Lingering awhile, the land to view,
'Neath the sun we stand.

Jonathan Field

*This poem is dedicated
in loving memory of
Dear Kit and Max.*

DEAR HEART

Time doth seem endless, for we are apart;
How can I live, when you have my heart?
The clock on the wall, ticks the minutes away,
Such precious moments, oh, please don't delay!

Come back to these arms, awaiting for you,
My love overfloweth, there is no-one but you!
You taught me to love you, I gave you my heart,
Please do not break it! How long must we part?

Tear down these walls dear, take me to thy side,
The love here within me, I cannot hide.
Make me thine own, dear, that's all that I pray,
My darling my love grows, for you more each day.

And time doth seem endless, while we are apart,
How can I live, when you have my heart?

Jonathan Field

This poem is dedicated to
My dearest Harry.
We shall meet again one day in Heaven.

A PROMISE

Sometime in the future,
When the sun has gone to rest,
And you are seated in your chair,
That chair you love the best,
I'll come and sit beside you,
And gaze into your eye,
That twinkle I shall see there,
A code 'tween you and I.

Yes, sometime in the future,
When the stars adorn the sky,
Although I sit beside you,
No words need you and I -
Your presence gives me comfort,
You have the love I craved.
But how to tell you my dear one,
That me from death you saved?

But, sometime in the future,
When all is quiet and still,
And I am here beside you,
Just as is God's will,
I'll find the words I need to say,   .
To you, my love alone,
That I shall ever bless the day,
You made me yours alone.

Jonathan Field

This poem is dedicated
In the loving memory of my dear Bill.

MY SON

My son,
I wept...as you suffered in pain.
Feeling so helpless
I prayed yet again
Then....I thought of the Father
Who wept for His Son
As he hung on the cross
Til His work be done

My son,
I suffered along with you
For as the pain cut through
It reached me too!
And now...I rejoice
As you are set free
No longer to suffer
I look to see
The reason? The purpose?
Some good to behold!
Our faith is yet strengthened
And refined as gold

My son,
As we venture along life's way
Let us remember that glorious day
When Jesus was there
Our pain He did bear
As He carried us through
And filled us anew

My son,
Behold...our Father's Son
Your Brother, your Saviour....God's Holy One!

Sheila Finch

This poem is dedicated to
my dear son Matthew 1994

MOTHER AND DAUGHTER

When you first arrived you filled me with joy
A bundle of treasure I'd always enjoy
From a child to a woman you gave me such pride
From baby to toddler young girl to bride
A wonderful daughter through every year
A feeling of love whenever you're near
I'll take second place now that you're a wife
But you'll always be a bright light in my life.

You're a mother a teacher a nurse and a friend
A person on who I could always depend
A lady who rid me of all of my fears
A provider of love for so many years
Thank you for giving me such a nice day
I saw how you cried when Dad gave me away
Though I've married the man who I hoped for and prayed
My feelings for you Mum will not ever fade.

Bruce Fisher

THOUGHTS OF WHY

Why don't you show some love to me, like you once used to do?
You no longer hold me tight when I make love to you
Why don't I get that lovely smile when I walk in the door?
What's happened to the welcome kiss I used to get before
Why don't you come with me sometimes and have a drink or two?
Why is it being with my friends doesn't appeal to you?
Why do you sit there quietly just watching the TV?
Why not go and turn it off and come and talk to me?
Why can't we stop these boring nights and make a brand new start?
I may just end up leaving you and that would break your heart.

Why don't you show some love to me why wait till we're in bed?
Why don't you walk across the room and love me now instead?
Why do you never compliment my hard work or my looks?
Why take for granted I'm the one that cleans and irons and cooks?
Why do you never take me out but go out with your mates?
Why can't it be like it once was those special loving dates?
Why won't you sit down by my side while I watch the TV?
Why don't you hold me in your arms and gently cuddle me?
Why can't I see the love we had why did it disappear?
One day you'll come into our home and you won't find me here.

Bruce Fisher

THE LADY IN BLACK

She moved slowly down the busy street,
Shabbily dressed in black from head to feet.
The carrier bag she held was filled with bread,
Broken with loving care for the ducks she fed.

Somehow I can't forget the distinctive face,
So filled with strength, character and grace.
She had known better times, I'm sure,
Her memories locked away behind closed door.

I'll always remember the old lady in black,
With her notable stoop and very precious pack.
The ducks were her friends, her only pleasure,
She loved every single moment they spent together.

Valerie Gamble

*I often saw the old lady walking along the Stoney Stanton Road in
Coventry on her way to the Swanswell Pool with her precious pack.
I haven't seen her for a long time but would like
to dedicate this poem to her memory.*

MY FOREIGN FRIENDS

My first foreign friend was Joe from Mauritius;
I always thought that he was delicious.
He'd turn up at the office smart in a suit
And always wore plenty of Brut!

Next was Margaret who came from Grenada,
When I lived in Woking she was my neighbour.
She popped in for sugar on New Year's Day -
We called it 'First Footing' bringing good luck our way!

Marjorie from Jamaica drove past the planes
When she took us both shopping in Staines.
On our way home, when we hadn't gone far,
The man called out: - 'You've left your bag on the car!!!'

Another friend was Bebe from Nepal;
We'd perform a dance at the church hall.
Some-one said she had expressive hands
Just like the ladies from Eastern lands.

Norma and her family came from Bombay,
We met in '65 while on holiday.
Laughter and sadness, our hopes and fears;
We've shared a lot over many years.

Vik and his family - they're from Vietnam
And run our corner shop - I pop in for jam.
He moans he spends hours cooped up inside,
And when he goes out - it's to Lakeside!

These aren't all my friends, but there isn't the time
To write them each a story in rhyme.
So Nina, Jo, Qamar, Jag, Zak and Sue -
You're still my friends - I won't forget you.

Anne Green

MUM AND DAD!

Mum and Dad are ever so sweet,
They tickle our feet,
And make good things for us to eat.

Mum and Dad are loving,
Caring and kind to,
They take us to pantomimes,
Where we shout hiss and boo.

Mum and Dad take care of us,
They treat us with respect,
Help us do our homework,
So it ends up perfect.

In the summer holidays,
When we're not having fun,
We go swimming for the day,
Then buy an iced bun.

But when we are naughty children,
And don't do what we're told,
Don't put away our things,
They will possibly be sold.

If we carry on,
Doing things we shouldn't
We miss out on treats,
And then we wish we didn't.

Anne-Marie Hackett

J.D.

A teardrop shed by a guardian angel,
Weeping because the protected is fleeing,
But to a better place, far grander than that we know.
Dear friend, you are so precious to me, and so special to us all,
Take refuge my son and say not 'my work is done'
But confide in me and say with tears of joy,
'My life with Him has just begun.'
Do not relapse into a world of dreams,
For I am coming and am here to show you far better things.
Things that will let you soar above the stars
Escape man's insular way of thought,
I love you my child, be patient and wait
For in your heart is a deep-rooted desire,
Which I am willing to fulfil, just trust and believe
In my unfailing love.

Elizabeth Hallett

This poem is dedicated to
Jack Hallett

I WISH

I wish you were there when
I walked through the valley
When I felt stumbled and lowly

I wish you were there when
Clouds of sorrow abounded
And when the thunder of sadness sounded

I wish you were there
To hold me in your arms
And sing to me the comfort of the psalms

I wish you were there
In the full spring bloom
And when flowers die, wither and gloom

I wish you were there when
The moon poured its silver glory
And when the twinkling stars told their story

I wish you are there in summer and winter,
In Autumn and spring
To share whatever, this life may bring

I wish you are always beside me
To this I am holding fast
This is my first wish and the last

I wish you are there in my
Joy and sorrow
You are not here today, will you be there tomorrow?

Aruna Hamid

MY LITTLE SISTER

My little sister never really held me
Only in her heart
Times we had, good, bad, happy and sad
Treasured memories I have.
Now she holds someone precious in her arms,
Someone made from her, someone small.
A baby girl!
My little sister, little no more,
Treasured memories I have.

Jacqueline Harvey

*This poem is dedicated to
my sister Gillian Harvey*

JUST MEMORIES

At first there was a light.
Warm, free strands of sunlight,
Splashed across our lives.
She was a sun-touched dawn.

But now there is a darkness;
A depth of night that cannot be explained.

At first there was a warmth.
Embraced in her love,
We strolled through unending days.
She was a comfort, a tender, early bloom.

But now there is Winter;
An icy chill cuts harshly through our hopes.

At first there was a life.
A friend, a wife, a mother.
But now there is nothing...
Just memories.

Sarah Harwood

This poem is dedicated to the
loving memory of my mother
1952 - 1988

THE CENTENARIAN

Wrapped up warm I am quite content
Although I may look old and bent
My arms and legs only want to rest
While my head sinks slowly to my chest.

I cannot see, but I don't mind
For the folks around me are so kind
Their loving hands, and tender touch
Give me the care I need so much.

I like a little idle chat
Nothing to deep, just this and that.
I enjoy the meals brought to me
But best of all a cup of tea.

I have been a wife and busy mother
That was the past, now I want no bother.
Let me live my life out peacefully
Just being alive is enough for me.
I am very happy for you see
I live again in my memory.

Monica Jefferies

MY SUMMER QUEEN

It was so many years ago and my old mind is fading away
When I walked into our park to watch our rugby team at play
Was it you I spied, A lovely girl looking so young and so serene
Having a picnic with your mother on our lush village green.

We gazed at one another, you caught me in your stare
Your mother scolded you for being rude to that boy over there
You were quite angry with your mother and let go a little scream
You were a little vixen then, and I heard your name was Kathleen.

We were good friends soon after, you laughed and teased me with glee
I said you were the love of my life, you said that you loved me
You had blue eyes of summer, a complexion made of cream
I was young and ruddy then and you were going on sixteen.

How we roamed the valleys, and climbed the hills on high
We talked to the wild winds, we were one with the earth and sky
We were never apart for we loved each other and could not have been
We picked the wild berries of the mountains, we make a very good
Team.

As the summer flowers bloomed, you grew with them more lovely still
You teased me with other boys and you I many times wanted to kill
With you and the glorious summer I was lost in a lovely dream
Your mother took you away, it was like you had never been.

That summer was many years ago it has long gone and withered away
I am an old man now and soon in the deep earth I will lay
I think sometimes I see us climbing mountains, running on the village
Green
As when I was just a ruddy lad and you were my summer queen.

Richard Jones

*This poem is dedicated to
my special friend Kathleen*

LOVE ONE ANOTHER

'Love one another,' the Master said,
Feel for your sister and your brother
Compassion for their pain.
And in their hopes and fears share, too;
Who knows when a thought of love for you
May heal your wounds and calm your mind;
Love one another, be kind.

Joyce Le Vicount

LIFE (OR THE LACK OF IT)

What is life?
When everything you own
Means less than nothing
When you are left alone
The things you share
The joys - the pleasures too
Even sadness - heartaches
But we pulled through.

But now she's gone
And sharing there is none
How can you share
When you are only one
Now I'm just waiting
For my time to go
So I can share again
With her - my joys and woe.

Walter Lee-Kitchin

SUCH LOVE

Such love - the depth of Your Love
the deep, deep depth of Your Love
for mankind through the ages.
It is passed our understanding,
how You have gone on loving and giving
despite, or maybe, because
of us and our
attitudes and actions to each other
and to You.

You gave us Leaders, Judges, Prophets, Kings
we heeded not.
Then You sent Your only Son, beloved of You
and we **crucified** Him!

It is hard to comprehend
What it means to love as You love.
'It demands my all, soul, life,
Goods, house, children, wife.'
All that I have, all that I am
I give to You.
Let me not withhold anything, for nothing
is too little to be offered - surrendered
to Your Love.
for You gave all - one complete and perfect sacrifice
out from the depths of Your Love
for us.

Mary-Joan Lloyd

DISCONNECTING CONTOURS

We meet again
Two disconnecting contours,
Living intangible lives.
The intricate spell has broken
The chemistry dissolves.

Discerning glances,
Replace the ready smiles.
Our reminiscences now,
Are little comfort to us both.
I've learnt to live without you
Can you live without me too?
We never really were one,
We never really could be.

Karen Marks

THIS FEELING

This feeling inside me
Will not go away
My love for you
Will always stay

To hear the words
'I love you'
I knew our love was true
Just to hear the three words from you.

You were always there for me
In every way
But what about me?
Was I there for you?

You're everything a girl could want in
A guy
And that's no lie
Your warm loving and kind
Thoughtful and caring too

There is no words in the world
Could tell how I feel for you
The flame of love inside
Burns for you forever.

Caroline Martin

This poem is dedicated to
all of my friends and loved ones,
who have played an important part in my life.
God bless you all.

REVERIE

Soft mists rising from the lake,
Caress the heart of one who aches
With longing for the far off times
When people listened to the chimes
Of peeling bells, on a Sunday morn,
But now the village is forlorn.

The children grew and went away,
To seek adventure, and to play
A different song on life's heartstrings.
So much to do, so many things
To lure the mind, to lead astray,
With whisperings of a better way.

They left the lake where gentle mists arise
And in the treetops kiss
The beckoning rays of a golden sun,
Lifting the spirit of the one
Who stands alone on that dreamtime shore,
With memories of time before,
When laughter sounded in the fells,
And on a Sunday, one heard bells.

Marilyn Michaels

This poem is dedicated to
my dearest children
Suzanne, Richard and Carolyn

FOR SARAH

When I was six weeks old,
For some reason known only to Himself,
God took you away.
You flew to Heaven on a June day,
When all unknowing, I slept in my cot
Beside an empty bed.
Oblivious, to what lay ahead of me.

Long, lonely years
Bereft of love, and you.
As I lived my life half a person,
I wondered,
About the sound of your voice,
Whether you liked to laugh,
And what was your favourite song?
Any little thing that I could glean about you,
Never was enough.
As time went by,
How I yearned for your presence.
I remember buying a Mother's Day card, to see
What it would be like,
To send you love, from me.
It was hard.
I have a picture that silently reflects your gaze.
As we look at one another,
I ponder at its sadness.

Did you know that you were soon to go,
And that you couldn't be my Mother?
I'm told that what you never have,
You never miss.
But still I would have liked the chance
To kiss
Your face,
And have a memory
Of your last embrace!

Marilyn Michaels

*This poem is dedicated to
my dearest Mother.
(1901 - 1933)*

MY GUY

I love the way you smile at me
Or hug me when I'm sad
What did I do to deserve you
You're the friend I never had

I used to think it wouldn't work
That you didn't love me so
But now I have you by my side
I'll never let you go

I have been moody, I have been wrong
But you put up with that
You put your arms around me tight
Just like your pussy cat

I now just want to thank you
For the times you've loved me so
Where would I be without you
Neither of us know

All I know is I love you
You're charming, friendly and kind
You have got your faults but haven't we all
It's not as if I mind

I really truly love you
I know you love me too
I've waited for you all my life
I know our love is true.

Helen Moore

67

DEATH CANNOT PART US

When you first departed from me,
my life also seemed to die.
A dungeon of darkness smothered me.
Numbness settled upon me.
Constant night seemed always in attendance.
Grief and loss weighed like a burden too heavy to bear.

But as February moved into March,
a flicker of response came as a snowdrop appeared in
fragile splendour.
The carpets of blue and white crocuses filled the gardens
and I remembered your joy at these jewels of creation.
My being struggled to escape from the dungeon of despair and
hopelessness,
to exchange the constant companion of sadness for the breathtaking
exclamations of joy we had shared each spring.
Bird song each morning heralded excitement for a new day and its
activities.
I could allow past memories and experiences we had shared
to enter my mind without heartache.
As the months pass you are so often a companion of my thoughts
and actions.
I am grateful for the happy times, the dreams and valleys we shared.
The wisdom and experiences you left as a bequest to me.
And although parted for a season-my mind and heart will always
treasure
and give thanks for the years we had together.

Grace Mowberry

LIFE IS A ROSE

Is not a rose but a long thorny stick
Crowned with a single beautiful bloom
Yet it has won a thousand hearts
And a single one can brighten a room
I believe that this world is like a rose
Filled with thorns that can cut like a knife
Crowned with a singular beautiful bloom
Hope the golden flower of life
I sometimes despair of the pain
When the thorns scratch me deep
I bleed and hurt yet not give up
I stay determined not to weep
For I was blessed with a magic rose
Crowned with not one bloom but two
Both flower deep within my heart
One is hope the other you.

Daniel Newland

*This poem is dedicated to
Sandra Rackley and Kelly Newman.
'Thanks for everything.'*

SHINE ON

Shine on sweet thing
You've so much joy and love to bring.
In your eyes a distant laughter rings,
In your heart a new and fresh song sings.

Lift your head up high
Lonely you need never be,
Deep breath in, and sigh
Just look around and you will see
So many people loving you, like me.

Wipe your eyes,
Watch my lips,
You're beautiful with so much to give.
I know your hurting,
I feel your pain,
Release the fear
And start to live again.

Sophy Newton

This poem is dedicated to Stephen

DEATH

Although we are now separate,
Although we are apart.
You are in all my memories,
You're always in my heart.

Death, it has come and taken you,
From my warm arms and soul.
I see you each and every day,
You make my being whole.

Your picture is beside our bed,
You have the pride and place.
I look at this picture every night,
I gaze into your face.

Your face is handsome, full of grace,
As it will always be.
I love you and I always will,
For all eternity.

Jon Nobes
.

PROMISES

Though love songs promise eternity,
I cannot make such claims,
The words I seek refuse me,
All love songs aren't the same.

I can't promise you forever,
Or a love till the end of time,
I'm no prophet, no fortune teller,
I know not how long you're mine.

For as we change with the world,
Time limits what we vow,
I can't say we won't grow cold,
Just I love you here and now.

Torsten Payne

MY PRICELESS MOTHER

I remember
My first day at nursery,
Not letting you go
Making you stay to watch me paint
You are my guardian angel, my mother

I remember
Leaving you for the first time
Sadness and fear swept past me
Even though it was for only one night

You made an impact on my life
That I can not even begin to thank you for
Your cheeky grin and bright blue eyes
Show you care

You will always be my hero, my mother
You were always there when the pain and heartache took over
I always could whisper a word in your ear and you would not
Laugh but shed a tear

From teaching me to talk to showing me you care
Is what you say
'Any mother would do'
But your love is stronger than that
And I am so grateful for you
My mother.

Lucy Peachey

This poem is dedicated to my Mum.
'Thanks for always being there for me.'

DEAR FATHER

The clock ticks quietly, almost silently
But to the girl
It pounds at her head,
Staring out of the window
Tears slide off her cheek,
The air is heavy from her pain
She turns her head glancing at the picture of the man
Who once,
Was her loving father,
Closing her eyes she dreams of yesterday
Yesterday
Where only her dreams can take her
Yesterday.

Lucy Peachey

'NEW FRIEND'

I have found a new friend,
A very special friend, he walks
With me, and he talks to me,
He is there when I am down.

He wipes my tears away, when I'm sad.
He washed away my sins.
He has shown me the right path to take.
He is always there for me.

His name is Jesus, Son of God.
A special friend to me.

Sue Perkins

ABSENT FRIEND

From childhood to adulthood it was always you and me
I remember all those Sunday School trips, when we went down to the
Sea
The nights when we slept over, and talked about our dreams
The type of men we'd one day marry was not long ago it seems.

There was a break - when we went our separate ways
But when we met up it seemed like only yesterday.
We both had got married and given birth to children too
And still our friendship remained steadfast, staunch and true.

And then one day you left us, God called you to his fold
No longer when I'm upset can I turn to you to hold
To feel your arms around me and tell me everythings alright.
You was on your way to me, they say, on that fateful night,
The night a drunken driver put out your loving light.

My dearest friend of yesterday, I'm left here all alone,
I sit beside your grave with my head upon the stone.
Your husband and your children can't make sense of how you died
Because a selfish being didn't think, and chose to drink and drive.

What will I do without you, my dearest friend, my all,
I'm dropping in a dark, dark pit and I can't seem to stop the fall.
Eventually I'll make new friends and get back my normal life,
Always we'll remember you as a friend, mother and wife.

When I look up in the sky upon the brightest star
I send a secret prayer to you and pretend you're not that far,
Wait for me my friend, for we'll be together again one day
The day that God decides, it's my turn to go away.

Amanda Potter

MY FAITHFUL FRIEND

His eyes were large soft and brown
Set below a golden crown
His love and loyalty knew no bounds
Always alert to the slightest sounds

Coming home in the evening from a hard days toil
He was always waiting, oh! so loyal
Tail awagging, eyes so bright
In the darkest of days, he was my light

Guarding me both day and night
Ready to stand his ground and fight
To protect me from any unseen danger
He patrolled the house like a lone ranger

I loved him so with all my heart
I died inside when we had to part
I'll miss the kisses he so readily gave me
And the weight of his head resting on my knee

The unconditional love that had no end
My tears fell in torrents when I had to tend
A leg that just would not heal on its own
The fear in my heart had grown and grown

As I knew I was losing our last fight together
And no matter how hard I tried God was taking you whatever
My Dearest Sabre, forgive me, I could see you suffer no more
I am now lost and alone, as I face a closed door.

My Soul Mate has gone to a far greater place
And all I have left is memories of his face

Wait for me Sabre, I'll be with you one day
And then again, my faithful friend, for eternity we can play
I'll love you forever, till there is no mankind
And we meet up again in another time.

For 10½ years you served me with devotion
With a heart full of love as big as the ocean
My heart will always remain faithful and true
My loyalties, like yours, will never stray from you.

Amanda Potter

*This poem is dedicated to
the memory of the best friend I ever had.
I'll never forget or stop loving you.
Till we meet again.*

GEORGE

We laughed and we loved,
We shared sorrow and joy,
God blessed our love,
With a girl and a boy.

He allowed us to share,
A love that was strong.
And I always believed,
It would go on and on.

But now you have gone George,
And life's not the same,
I wake every morning,
My heart filled with pain.

So George can you help,
To carry me through,
Each new day that dawns,
Until I'm with you.

Gill Powell

This poem is dedicated to Peggy

DES

Oh Des, how I loved you
If only you'd known,
And now that you've gone,
I'm so <u>very</u> alone.

My anger subsided,
The day that you died,
Too late to tell you,
Oh Des, <u>how</u> I've cried.

So many regrets,
About words never said,
Words that kept swirling,
Around in my head.

Too late now to tell you,
How great was my love,
But Des, you must know now,
In God's Heaven Above.

Gill Powell

This poem is dedicated to
a very special person

REGRETS

I've lost my only Uncle
He's up in Heaven above,
I always thought he'd be here,
So I never showed my love.

Too late to say 'I love you'
Too late to say 'I care.'
Too late to ever let him know,
I thought he'd always be there.

Too late to go and see him,
Too late to say 'get well,'
Too late to see him one more time,
To say a sad farewell.

I hope he has forgiven me,
Because I loved him so,
He was my only Uncle,
My regret, he had to go.

Gill Powell

*This poem is dedicated to
my uncle Ken*

MY DREAM

I had a dream the other night,
. Yet in my heart I feel,
It wasn't really just a dream,
In fact, it was quite real.

I was sitting in my armchair,
Feeling rather sad,
When suddenly a knock on my door,
And standing there was my dad.

'Oh hello dad' I said to him,
He came in and just sat down,
'It seems ages since I've seen you'
He just looked at me with a frown.

'Well I've just called in to see you love'
'And tell you not to weep'
'I'm in God's Heaven up above,
In a deep and wonderful sleep.'

'But dad, we want you back again,'
'To surround us with your love'
'I'm glad your safe in Heaven,'
'But we're not with you up above.'

He looked at me and softly smiled,
And in my heart I know,
He'd come to see me one last time,
Now I had to let him go.

He slowly got up from the chair,
I knew he couldn't stay,
He gently squeezed my hand in his,
And slowly slipped away.

When I think about that dream I had,
I just feel full of love,
Because now I know he's with me,
Watching down from up above.

Gill Powell

This poem is dedicated to the
Loving memory of my dad

STICKY TOFFEE!

I think of this like de'ja'vu,
And stupidly I fall for you,
The fun we had a year ago,
I long for, like you'd never know.

When you asked I soon refused,
But after that I felt confused,
It started off with just a kiss,
And after that was almost bliss.

Those summer days I won't forget,
You said, the end, you still regret,
We had such fun, this time, last year,
And now you come and reappear.

You said your heart still beats for me,
But you and I just cannot be,
No matter how I want it too,
It's something I just cannot do.

Clare Pritchard

LONELY LIFE

In this hazy, smoke-filled public bar,
Pint in hand, I wonder
Why fates cruel hand has deigned
To rend our love asunder.
Around me peals of laughter
Mock the happiness I knew,
And salty tears course down my face
'Cause I'm not here with you.
Why are we not together?
My grieving soul does ask,
While all those that surround me
Smile, as in their love they bask.
I don't expect life to be fair
Or treat me specially,
But is to share such happiness
To desperate a plea?
I must be the only soul
To suffer this cruel ill,
Unable to feel loves caress
And to your touches thrill.
Perhaps I should just up and leave
These happy folk alone,
Make my way back to the prison
Of my bleak and empty home.

Nigel Purssell

UNREQUITED LOVE

There's no void that's as great or deep
· As unrequited love,
There's no hole that is blacker
In the universe above.
The emptiness can't be described
Of a heart forever true,
Despairing, crying out in pain
'Why can't you love me too?'

A lonely heart needs tenderness
But more importantly,
It needs to feel of us to you,
Meet all your needs, you see;
Satisfy each wish and whim,
Fill your soul with glee,
Hold you in its body's arms,
Satisfy you sexually.

There's nothing that's perverted
In caring in this way,
When a heart has found its perfect mate
Forever and a day.
And though it finds that you prefer
Anothers arms instead,
It cannot give up trying as
Alone it would be dead.

So please forgive, O lady fair,
The attention that I give.
Ignore if I am jealous
If you turn elsewhere to live.
The life you let me glimpse before
Your spell on me you wove,
For there's no void that's as great or deep
As unrequited love.

Nigel Purssell

CUTIES

Bless their little cotton socks
Bless their little suities,
Bless their faces, feet and hands,
Our babies, little cuties!

When they're awake, they crawl, they climb
They sit back with their looties,
Some scissors and a half bald cat,
Shorn by these little cuties!

They scream, they cry, they whine, they bawl
They chew their little booties,
'Til they get everything they want,
Precocious little cuties!

We feed them, clothe them, care for them
Do all our little duties,
God bless them most when they're asleep,
Angelic little cuties!

Joyce Rafferty

FRIENDSHIP

Friendship is foreign these days,
Appreciation is alien.
It's not often you find a river in your mind
Belonging to someone else.

Something's hurting inside,
As it pushes to be released
The force is pathetic,
And emotions are teased.

The last tear is saved for you,
To form and fall on the solid rock,
And moisten the surface,
To help wind a slowing clock.

A permanent fixture,
Until weather wears it away.
But even rocks don't last forever,
We'll say bye bye one day.

Words are weird,
Psychology is misleading.
Only aliens understand,
The others thinking and feeling.

Interpreting what's inside,
Not what's written on this page,
Makes you my best friend,
And my rock on God's stage.

Konce Ramadan

This poem is dedicated to
Sonal and Harleen...
...Smile, I'll always be there. XX

THE OLD CLOCK

Moments passing all the time
Making memories with each chime
Happy groom and happy bride
By your side, how I shared your pride.

Look into my face
How can time replace
Days with you when I was new
And you were dressed in lace.

Noon and midnight every day
Hands together I would pray,
Turning winter into spring
From the day you wore your wedding ring.

I have served you very well
Age is silencing my bell
Now my wheels are turning slow
Will I stop? Will I go? - Time will tell.

I've journeyed through my time with you
But now I've reached the end
Yet in your dreams you'll see my face
Your old familiar friend.

Your life goes on without me
In your minds you'll hear my chime
And in this special way we'll be
Together all the time.

Carol Ratcliffe

This poem is dedicated to
my dear parents, Lily and Ted Amey
on the occasion of their 60th Wedding Anniversary
and to Albert for writing the music.

I REMEMBER

I remember Grandma
Always generous and kind,
Someone to replace you
I simply cannot find.

I remember Grandad,
With a sparkle in your eye,
Always pleased to see me
I never liked to say good bye.

I remember Auntie Wendy,
And the fact you liked to draw,
We shared some happy moments,
I wish there could have been more.

I remember Uncle Paul,
You didn't have much to say,
But now that I am older,
I know it was just your way.

I remember Uncle Colin,
Always happy and such fun,
When you walked inside a room,
Along walked in the sun.

I dedicate this poem,
To all of the above,
I'm sorry that I've lost you all
And send you all my love.

Nicki Rhodes-Foster

THREE RINGS

Three rings has been our code now
For nearly twelve long years
It started for a reason
When Dad left us both in tears

Although he may be gone now
It hasn't changed a thing
Of how I feel towards you
And for all the joy you bring

Then as we both get older
You'll never be alone
Because dear Mum I'll always be
Right next to my old phone

There barely goes a second
Without a thought of you
And I cannot be happy
If I know that you are blue

I can be with you in minutes
Be it night or day
You only have to call me
And I'll be right on my way

So when I tell you that I love you
It comes straight from my heart
And I hope and pray dear Mother
That we will never part

Anne E. Roberts

This poem is dedicated to
my Mum Beryl Winifred Roberts.
In memory of my Dad Lawrence Henry Roberts
(9.5.85)

MEMORIES

Memories are treasures
. No one can take away
They are ours forever,
Forever, come what may.

In nostalgic quiet moments
Or dreamy reverie,
To pause awhile
A laugh, a smile,
A tear or two maybe.

Memories are treasures
No one can take away.
The staff of life forever,
Forever, come what may.

Ted Rogers

MY SISTER

I feel so close almost as one
Secrets shared mingled with fun
Our thoughts collide time and again
Laughter and tears sorrow and pain.

We are two people living apart
Thoughts entwined so close at heart
I pick up the phone your number I dial
When the phone goes down I'm left with a smile.

Always ready to listen you always care
Who would I turn to if you were not there?
We often talk for hours on end
Problems to solve hearts to mend.

I'll always be there to share your pain
We'll sit and talk till we can smile again
If we should be parted what would I do
How could I cope without someone like you?

You are my only one no more to be had
Of the one that I have I am Oh so glad
You are my sister and will always be
So close to my heart you are a part of me.

Sharon Rosenwould

AS SHE CLOSED HER EYES

She closed her eyes
To this world of ours
Having looked beyond the fears
The golden light of life to come
Had wiped away the tears

She said her 'Goodbyes'
In her own way
With memories flooding by
Feeling so peaceful and content
There was no need to cry

She had made her mark
In the book of Life
Never to be erased
With open arms and welcoming smiles
They greeted her to happy days

The sun so bold
The flowers so bright
The atmosphere so pure
The overwhelming beauty
Almost too much to endure

With youthful zest
And pain free rush
Relief began to realise
This heavenly place now home
As she closed her eyes

She closed her eyes
And then with ease
Slipped beyond the door
The brightness and the beauty
Never imagined before

Sharon Rosenwould

MEMORIES

Down the trail of memories
Along the path we trod,
My thoughts will always be of you,
Each time I pray to God.

I'll pray that He will bless you,
And make your pathway fair,
Because my darling, in my heart,
You always will be there.

And although my heart be breaking,
And many tears will flow,
I'll think of all the happiness,
You gave me long ago.

And as the lonely years go by,
I shall be wondering too,
If you will sometimes think of me,
Because I loved you so.

And wherever life's pathway leads you,
Along the troubled way,
I hope my own beloved,
We'll meet again someday.

Sheelagh Royall

This poem is dedicated to
Frank Sandall

THOSE WERE THE DAYS

The land was deserted where the rain used to run
Grey was the sky, and the children at home
Sat wistfully eyeing the scene - full of woe,
Thinking of past times, long long ago.

Times when the sun had just peeped through the clouds.
Cheekily grinning down at the crowds.
Times when the river had run its full course
When the farmer had kept a dappled grey horse.

The little wood hut had been perched on the hill
And people sometimes walk there still.
But all that is left is a small epitaph
Reminding the watchers again of the past.

Past days when they too used to be young
And building mud pies used to be such fun.
But now in a cottage they sit in the warm
No longer enjoying a chase with the storm.

They think of the children who now have the time
To go out from the fire, to run, jump and climb.
Enjoying themselves with their lives stretched ahead
Then drowsily crawling back home to their bed.

With the past all behind them and nothing to lose
Time can be taken to do just as they choose.
Watching the children playing out in the rain,
Memories behind - to repeat once again.

Carol Scanlon

DIANE AND NORMAN

Today at last you pledge your love.
Though a short time previous you were hardly friends
By midday on this day
You shall be husband and wife.

The 16th of September, a day to mark the love you share.
A reminder that cupid set his sights on the both of you
Though you had no idea
That you were the target of his arrow.

Your wedding on a Saturday.
A day of harmony to lead to years
The beginning of the life you are to have together
Twenty-four hours that will remain so memorable.

Eleven-forty, the time at which you declare 'I do.'
A moment witnessed by many
That will never be forgotten
Simple words to become your most treasured.

Diane and Norman - a couple.
You two so perfectly matched
Made for each other and brought together by chance
To fall in love and marry on this day.

And on this day you take your vows.
I leave little more to say
Only to congratulate the both of you
And wish you happiness always and on your wedding day.

Kirby Scott-Horne

This poem is dedicated to
my dear friend Diane.
With love to you always.

CHILDLESS

How wonderful I cry as I first see her baby boy,
She kisses his cheek and strokes his tiny fingers.
My heart tightens as I place into his hand a fluffy toy.
Hot tears prick and sting behind my heavy tear tired eyes.

Do you not know what this is doing to me, my mind cries.
I walk home in a fog, trying hard not to think.
The feel of that small form still lingers in my arms.
Next time it will be okay, frantically I clean the sink.

My hopes rise allowing myself again to begin to believe.
A cot, a pram, little things to buy and knit.
This heart of mine fills full of hope anew.
Why not this time, I sit allowing myself to dream.

Catching my breath as days creep slowly on, and on.
Let it be this time, echo's of longing from deep inside.
Then hopes are dashed, my dreams are gone.
Peep behind the curtain as my friend goes by.
Cannot face her today, do not even want to try.

Vanessa Sherwood

STORMS

I sat for a while, deep in thought,
The skies turned cloudy and grey,
Reflecting on the times we had
But that was yesterday.

A crack of thunder lights up the sky
A storm is stirring so fine,
I never knew that so many storms
Were concealed in this heart of mine.

Kim Singh

FRIENDS

Oh grandad how we miss you, dear old Ben and me.
You died and left us lonely, we had so much fun you see,
We did not realise that your time had come so fast.
For Ben was just a puppy then and I thought it all would last.
Time has come around once more Ben and I are older too.
I am now thinking of the years when we had a friend in you.
I see so clear those sunny days we never had a care.
But the little house we lived in by the sea, it is not there.
I still recall the winter nights when the bitter wind would howl.
We sat cosy round the old log fire while you would tell a tale,
Of big tall ships and pirates all fighting under sail.
You would talk for hours and Ben would wake and nod his little head.
I knew the time was coming when you would send me off to bed.
You would come along and tuck me in and softly say goodnight.
I said my prayers with tight shut eyes then drift off on my flight.
On dragons wings I would soar so high I thought it rather neat.
There was no fear or dangers with Ben sleeping at my feet.
When morning came we were up and off down to the sandy shore.
To play more games and have more fun as we did many times before.
I remember well the time I fell my knee grazed on a rock.
I laughed as you bent to help me with Ben chewing on your sock.
Yes those funny treasured moments will be with me till I die.
But poor old Ben can't understand or know the reasons why.
But I know that he is thinking that if he could open doors.
Some day we will be together again to play on distant shores.
I am sitting by the fire staring right into the flames.
I am certain that I see you laughing playing funny games.
I never will forget you Grandad and I know again we will meet.
But for now I have contentment with dear old Ben here at my feet.

William Singleton

100

A SHADOW AWAY

My dear love has died.
Bitter tears I've cried
Feeling no relief
In my hours of grief.

Memories return
To torment and burn
Pictures in my brain;
Tears flow once again.

With a tender glance
He made my heart dance,
How could we foresee
That he would leave me?

No more laughing eyes
Watching my surprise
When each thought we shared
Showed how much we cared.

One day there will be
An answer for me
Why he died so young
Life's tune not yet sung.

No words can erase
These sad, empty days
But he'll still be near
No presence more dear.

So I'll smile again
Rejecting the pain
For he lives today
Just shadows away.

Joan Stangroom

THE LAUGHING STOPS

In my house there used to be people laughing happily
But now there's no more laughing just shedding of the
Tears, that every one has shared throughout this awful year.

When someone's here you love and its hard to say you care
You wished that you had told them that you really care.

But now there's something missing and its hard
To understand, that the brother that I loved so much is resting in
God's hands.

Nicola Stewart

This poem is dedicated to
my brother Mark, forever in my dreams

A PART OF ME DIED

'I'm pregnant,' she told me, it wasn't planned it came all too soon
Deep down I was overwhelmed, I was over the moon
It was a fantastic feeling I felt so proud
I wanted to shout it from the roof tops, and scream it out loud.
A proud father I was going to be
My joy, I wanted the world to see.
So used to looking after number one
Now I'm gonna have a daughter or a son.

It was a dream come true, it was all I ever wanted
And to top it all in another month we are getting wed.
A wife and child on the way
Husband and family man, what more can I say
Would it be a girl? Would it be a boy?
I don't care what it is, its gonna be my pride and joy.

Driver twenty get to the hospital your wife is waiting outside,
I can still picture her face and the tears she cried.
It was supposed to be a routine check up, but I knew something was
Wrong.
Its heart had stopped beating, it was only four inches long.
Yes we lost the baby, we were both devastated.
My wife had a D.N.C., the pregnancy was terminated.

She was carrying my child, that day a part of me died.
I had to be strong, but secretly I cried.
That was all in the past and here we are in the present.
Still only two of us, maybe it was all meant
There could have been three of us now, a complete family.
I, my wife and our four year old child, obviously it was not meant
To be.

Brian Stoneman

This poem is dedicated to my wife Kelly.
It was a very traumatic and upsetting time, but we came through it.
The secret is never indulge in self pity, there is always
someone worse off than you.

THE LOVERS

Scarce we talked of love
Scarce we talked at all

I would scan the paper
While you got the tea
Or prune my roses
While you watched me
Out of the corner of one eye
At your herbaceous border
Busy with a trowel

Scarce we talked of love
Scarce we talked at all

I would fix whatever
While you made us a cuppa
And when I'd finished
We would sip comfortably
In our favourite places
Glancing up now and then to
Read each other's faces

Scarce we talked of love
Scarce we talked at all

Now I prattle away
In a misty rain
Bring you roses where you lie
In a patch of cemetery
Song birds for company
Wondering - why?
Again, again

Scarce we talked of love
Scarce we talked at all

Roger N Taber

104

THE ROSE

Your scent is carried upon the air
Nature created you with loving care
Shaping each petal, like a work of art
Enclosed around your centre your heart.

An artist palette can not compare
With your beautiful colours, which you let us share
Upon your stem you carry a thorn
Protecting your heart from the day you were born,

And when your last days are due
Your beauty does not desert you
You shed your petals upon the ground
And kiss it gently without a sound.

Your scent still carried upon the air
You thing of beauty with no compare.

William Tremlett

ANOTHER NEW YEAR

I'll light a candle to you my love.
At this special time of year.
And send a blood red rose to the one
I still hold dear.

As I raise a glass of merry cheer to
Toast Auld Lang Syne.
My mind will take me back to a time,
When you were mine.

Eagerly with thumping heart I'll pass,
Through the veil of time.
And there in dreams of yester-year again
You will be mine.

Leslie Velvin

TIMELESS

It all began some time ago.
Sparked by a moment opportune.
The friends could not hope to predict, though,
Their actions fascinating beyond the moon.

He was backward in coming forward,
She just couldn't be sure.
The emotional fire kept gaining more wood,
While thoughts and deeds remained but pure.

Coming home together, one event-filled night,
As was then the fashion,
The two - him, every cheery, her, young and bright,
Happened upon a night of passion.

Her hair blazed a fiery red,
His eyes shone an earthly dark.
The two united on a single bed,
Branding both an indelible mark.

The common link had thus been fused,
The bond between them strong.
Both, however, somewhat confused,
The path ahead visibly long.

A second union did little to alter
The uneasy situation.
Both parties in solutions faltered,
Giving rise to complication.

He thought he cared more than she should know,
Hoping, bravely, that things could be resolved.
It turned into an uncomfortable show,
Neither sure of the others involve.

He, the romantic, raring to go,
She, the frantic, unsure as yet
The story parodies that of a Romeo,
And, perhaps, his fair Juliet.

Adam J.K. Ward

This poem is dedicated to
Claire, with timeless love and thanks.

VOICE ON THE WIND

If I should die before you,
I'll watch you from above.
I'll keep you safe in all you do,
Remember this my love.

You'll hear my voice on the
Wind cry out, I'll never be far away
As you lay your head on the
Pillow at night, weary from
Work of the day.

Don't mourn for me when I'm not there,
Place your hands together in a prayer.
Your name I'll whisper, so that you will know.
How very much I loved you so.

Holli Wells

WHO DO YOU SEE WHEN YOU LOOK AT ME

What do you see, tell me, what do you see?
Who are you seeing when looking at me?
A crabbed old woman, not very wise -
Uncertain of habit, with far-away eyes
Who seems not to notice the things that you do
And forever is losing a stocking or shoe?
Is that what you're thinking, is that what you see?
Then open your eyes for you're not seeing me.
I'll say who I am as I sit here so still,
As I rise at your bidding and eat at your will:
I'm a small child of 10 with a father and mother,
Sisters and brothers who love one another.
A young girl of 16 with wings on her feet
And dreaming that soon her true sweetheart she'll meet.
A bride at just 20 my heart gives a leap
When remembering the vows I promised to keep
At 25 now I have bairns of my own
Who need me to build a secure happy home.
A woman of 30, my children grow fast,
Bound to each other with ties that should last.
At 40 my grown sons soon will be gone
But my man stays beside me to see I don't mourn
At 50 once more babies play at my knee -
Again we know children, my loved one and me.
Dark days are upon me, my husband is dead;
I look at the future and I shudder with dread.

My children are busy with bairns of their own
While I think of the years and the love I have known
I'm an old woman now, grace and vigour depart
But thousands of memories still live in my heart
Inside it, you see, a girl therein dwells
And now and again my tired heart swells
I remember the joy, I think of the pain
And I'm loving and living life over again.
So open your eyes, please, open and see
Not a crabbed old woman, look closer and see me.

Kathleen Westwood

I KNOW HOW YOU WATCH ME

I sleep in your arms but I dream of the days
Of a love long, long gone by.
You hear me breathe, and you do not know
That I know how you watch me lie.

So I hear your words in my head at night,
(For you think you know me well) -
How your plans for love have all come true,
But for me they sound the knell

For a love, for a love that cries once more
To be remembered, felt, endured;
A love that was buried, lies cold and old,
Yet daily fresh immured.

And in the day, cold light of day,
Such thoughts are kept at bay;
But in your arms, each dreaded night,
The memories hold sway.

I know how you watch me as I lie,
Feigning sweet, untroubled sleep.
But in despair I remember him,
Whose love lies fathoms deep.

So I sleep in your arms, but still dream of the days
Of a love long, long gone by;
You think you know all there is to know
But I know how you watch me lie.

Alex Wilde

I STILL DON'T UNDERSTAND

I don't understand why you came,
Or why you left without saying goodbye.
For now that you've gone, nothings the same,
And all I seem to do is cry.
Until the day that I'm by your side,
My heart will never feel complete.
As you are the pain I can not hide,
The sole object of loves defeat.
Touch my aching heart, be my shining light,
And whisper comforts to my ears.
Watch over me throughout the night
And guide me through my years.
Look down on me from up above
And help me to understand you with love.

Anthony Williams

YOUR GARDEN

Your garden still, with signs of life anew
Still breathes and blooms with warmth entwined with you.
Though our tender hand no longer cares and nurtures,
Still endlessly the snowdrops grace each spring
As though the love you gave, lives on for you.
And ever will the bluebells bow their heads
In sadness of the loss your garden feels.
For all the beauty held within each bloom
Could not replace the beauty found in you.
And still your chair sits patiently awaiting
Through April showers and autumn leaves that fall
Knowing, that sadly, you've been taken.
Yet.
In presence you have never left at all.

Marie Williams

*Dedicated in loving memory of my Grandfather, Roland Williams,
lovingly called Roly Poly. He is deeply missed and remains with us
in the hearts of his family.*

COLOUR

If we take the time to look, everywhere we'll see
The colours of the rainbow in flowers, trees and sea
So often we just hurry on, looking straight ahead,
But take a moment longer, and look around instead.

The pastel shades of blossom upon the tress in spring,
Dainty bluebells in the wood, and yellow that daffodils bring,
Then brighter hues of summer flowers, and gold when the harvest's
Due,
Deep velvety green of a new mown lawn, and the red of a sunset too.

Those beautiful colours of autumn when the leaves begin to fall,
How can we just ignore them, not seeing them at all?
Even on a winter's day there is colour to be found
With the sparkle of a heavy frost, and snow upon the ground.

So take a look around at the colour everywhere.
You can always find it, any time of year.
No matter what the season or what the time of day,
Colour will be waiting to brighten up your way.

Pam Williams

GOD MADE MY WISH COME TRUE...

I could never wish for a better mother,
Than the one God gave to me.
I'm so glad she's always loved me,
Because I love her wholeheartedly.
She's done her very best for me,
When my father left, she brought me up alone.
I'm so very proud of her,
Because she never thought to moan.

When I grew up I wished that God,
Would give me a husband to marry.
And I hoped that he wouldn't,
Disregard its importance and choose to dally.
As years went by, I thought my wish ...
Well, I thought it would never come true.
But then suddenly, surprisingly -
Miraculously - I met you!

I'm so glad that you're my husband,
And that God made my wish come true.
I love you with all my heart,
And I love my dear mother too.
I've wished for many things in life,
Mostly they weren't wishes for myself.
But I'm so very happy God didn't leave me,
Unmarried, and residing on that <u>notorious shelf</u>.

Sheryl Williamson

*This poem is dedicated to
my loving husband Scott.*

LOST LOVE

When you fall in love
You feel just fine,
Just like your first taste
Of a mature, sweet wine.
It makes your skin tingle,
It makes your skin glow,
And you think of your loved one
Where-ever you go.
But when your love leaves
You can't bear the truth,
You sigh and you listen
In the long, lonely hush
For the sound of his footstep -
For the sound of his voice -
You can't believe it's over:
There's no reason to rejoice.
You wonder what went wrong,
You wonder where you erred,
You find it hard to believe
It was what you wanted you heard.
His face is a shadowy vision,
His touch a sweet memory,
His voice a long, low whisper
Of what you thought might be.
You still can hear the echo
Of thoughts that passed between -
The feel, the touch, the taste of him -
Which you hope will be evergreen.

Shirley Woodbridge